We Use Water

by Robin Nelson

first step nonfiction

Lerner Publications Company · Minneapolis

We use water every day.

We drink water.

We use water to cook.

We make ice **cubes**
with water.

We use water to grow food.

We grow flowers with water.

We use water to
keep clean.

We wash the car with water.

We use water to **sail** boats.

We fish in water.

We use water to build
sand castles.

We swim in water.

Firefighters use water to
put out fires.

Ships go places on water.

We use water to
make **electricity.**

There are so many ways
to use water!

The Earth's Water

We cannot drink most of the earth's water. The pie graph on page 19 shows all the water on the earth. The green part of the graph is salt water that is in the oceans. We do not drink or use salt water. The white part of the graph is fresh water that is frozen in ice caps and glaciers. We cannot use this water either. The blue part of the graph is the smallest. This is fresh water that we can use for drinking, washing, and other needs.

Fresh Water

Frozen Water

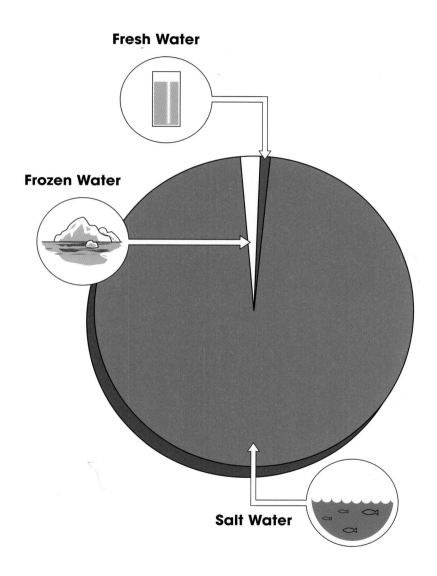

Salt Water

Using Water Facts

It takes about 39,000 gallons of water to make a new car and its four tires.

It takes about 1,500 gallons of water to make a fast food meal of a hamburger, french fries, and a soda. This includes water used to grow the potatoes, to grow the grain for the bun, to grow the grain to feed the cows, and to make the soda.

A bath uses about 36 gallons of water.

A toilet uses 5 to 7 gallons of water for every flush.

A leaky faucet can waste up to 100 gallons of water a day.

Turn off the faucet while you brush your teeth. You could save up to 5 gallons of water a day!

Glossary

 cubes – solid objects with six sides

 electricity – energy that gives us power and makes things work

 firefighters – people who put out fires

 sail – to make a boat move with wind

 ships – big boats that travel through deep water

Index

cook – 4

electricity – 16

firefighters – 14

fish – 11

flowers – 7

food – 6

ships – 15

swim – 13

The photographs in this book are reproduced through the courtesy of: PhotoDisc, front cover, pp. 7, 9; © Diane Meyer, p. 2; © Larry & Rebecca Javorsky/Photo Agora, p. 3; © Todd Strand/ Independent Picture Service, pp. 4, 5, 22 (top); © Stephen Graham Photography, pp. 6, 10, 13, 15, 17, 22 (second from bottom, bottom); © Robert Maust/Photo Agora, pp. 8, 12; Stockbyte, p. 11; © Wes Harman/Photo Agora, pp. 14, 22 (middle); OPIC, pp. 16, 22 (second from top).

Illustration on page 19 is by Tim Seeley.

Lerner Publications Company
A division of Lerner Publishing Group
241 First Avenue North
Minneapolis, MN 55401 USA

Website address: www.lernerbooks.com

Library of Congress Cataloging-in-Publication Data

Nelson, Robin, 1971–
    We use water / by Robin Nelson.
        p.   cm. — (First step nonfiction)
    Includes index.
    ISBN: 0–8225–4594–2 (lib. bdg. : alk. paper)
    1. Water use—Juvenile literature. 2. Water-supply—Juvenile literature. I. Title. II. Series.
TD348 .N45 2003
553.7—dc21   2002007191

Manufactured in the United States of America
1 2 3 4 5 6 – JR – 08 07 06 05 04 03